Delivering affordable housing through Section 106

Delivering affordable housing through Section 106

Outputs and outcomes

Sarah Monk, Tony Crook, Diane Lister, Roland Lovatt, Aoife Ni Luanaigh, Steven Rowley and Christine Whitehead

JOSEPH ROWNTREE
FOUNDATION

The **Joseph Rowntree Foundation** has supported this project as part of its programme of research and innovative development projects, which it hopes will be of value to policy makers, practitioners and service users. The facts presented and views expressed in this report are, however, those of the authors and not necessarily those of the Foundation.

Joseph Rowntree Foundation
The Homestead
40 Water End
York YO30 6WP
Website: www.jrf.org.uk

© University of Cambridge 2006

First published 2006 by the Joseph Rowntree Foundation

ISBN–13: 978 1 85935 468 1
ISBN–10: 1 85935 468 8

A pdf version of this publication is available from the JRF website (www.jrf.org.uk).

A CIP catalogue record for this report is available from the British Library.

Cover design by Adkins Design

Prepared and printed by:
York Publishing Services Ltd
64 Hallfield Road
Layerthorpe
York YO31 7ZQ
Tel: 01904 430033; Fax: 01904 430868; Website: www.yps-publishing.co.uk

Further copies of this report, or any other JRF publication, can be obtained either from the JRF website (www.jrf.org.uk/bookshop/) or from our distributor, York Publishing Services Ltd, at the above address.

Contents

1 The research question

What is the issue?

A significant proportion of the affordable housing required to meet need over the next decade will be delivered through the land use planning system using Section 106 (S106) agreements. The Chancellor's response to the Barker Review (2004) suggests that these agreements should be restricted to a much narrower range of obligations than at present – those associated directly with the development and the provision of affordable housing. This should help to expand provision. On the other hand, the Government's continued emphasis on mixed communities means that there are likely to be very few 100 per cent affordable housing sites – the mainstay of past affordable housing provision (Monk *et al.*, 2005). This puts even greater emphasis on ensuring that the planning approach to providing affordable housing actually works well.

Yet little is known about how far the S106 policy actually delivers on the ground what has been specified in the legal agreement. Our previous work focused very much on the implementation of the overall policy and on the numbers of units agreed (Crook *et al.*, 2002; Monk *et al.*, 2005; Whitehead *et al.*, 2005). Anecdotal evidence, including from professional bodies and the major lobby and industry groups (see Chapter 2 of this report), suggests that there is considerable concern about whether agreements are being fully implemented.

In terms of ensuring the provision of affordable housing, signing an S106 agreement is only the starting point. First, not all planning permissions are actually built out, because they lapse, or they are duplicates or they are superseded – so neither the market nor the affordable housing is provided. Second, as development proceeds, further negotiations may mean that the original agreement is modified. As a result, what is actually delivered on an S106 site is not necessarily what is envisaged at the time of the negotiations associated with the granting of planning permission.

This report aims to help fill this gap in the evidence. It focuses on whether the delivery of affordable housing through S106 works in its own terms, i.e. the extent to which the affordable housing agreed is actually delivered. Only if the delivery stage works well can the policy be regarded as an effective means of meeting affordable housing requirements.

The legal and administrative parameters

The legal basis for achieving affordable housing lies in Section 106 of the Town and Country Planning Act 1990. This enables the negotiation of matters related to development, which are necessary if the development is to proceed but which may not be lawfully secured through placing conditions on planning permissions.

In the case of affordable housing, government policy has explicitly put in place the use of planning agreements to facilitate developers' contributions. Initially restricted to meeting rural housing needs, government policy now enables and encourages planning authorities to obtain contributions on all but small-scale residential development sites (DETR, 1998; ODPM, 2005a, 2005b).

Planning authorities do not have carte blanche when entering into these negotiations. First, they must have explicit policies about the provision of affordable housing in their local development frameworks backed up by up-to-date housing needs surveys. Second, policy endorses making the affordable housing contribution on the site for which the permission for the private development is sought in order to foster mixed communities. Third, where possible, the emphasis is placed on brownfield development as part of the Government's urban renaissance policy but with continued encouragement to seek affordable contributions on these as well as on greenfield sites. Fourth, the Government advises planning authorities to seek contributions only on sites above a specific threshold (sites with at least 15 dwellings outside inner London), although planning authorities may negotiate contributions on smaller sites if there are explicit local policies in place. The widespread use of thresholds effectively restricts the provision of affordable housing to sites that yield approximately half of total private sector completions.

Prior to entering into agreements, developers and local planning authorities negotiate (often at length) over the terms of the agreement, a matter of some concern in terms of lengthening the process of agreeing planning permission. The level of detail included in the obligation is itself a matter of negotiation. The concerns about the processes of negotiating S106 agreements in general apply as strongly to affordable housing negotiations and one of the Government's objectives has been to speed up the process, improve transparency and reduce uncertainty.

S106 agreements require developers to carry out specified obligations when implementing planning permissions. Obligations, including those specific to affordable housing, can be implemented either by providing what is needed to a standard specified in the agreement or by paying a sum to the planning authority, which will then itself provide the facility. The obligations are registered as local land charges and therefore successors in title are just as obliged to carry out the contract as the original party to the negotiations.

Once the S106 agreement has been signed it is a legally binding private contract that operates alongside the statutory planning permission. The fact that an agreement has been reached does not prevent developers or planning authorities seeking to modify it, either before or once development has commenced. Circumstances may have changed and rendered obsolete what was originally an acceptable obligation. The terms of S106 agreements can be amended with a deed of variation but any amendment must consider the same set of principles set out in government circulars. Affected parties can also apply to have agreements modified or discharged after five years, with a right of appeal if the local planning authority refuses to agree a modification.

Planning authorities have powers to enforce compliance with agreements. The extent to which this process can be effective depends not only on the details of the agreement but also on monitoring and enforcement capacity. Most fundamentally, these agreements are dependent on the development going ahead. There is no obligation unless the planning permission is taken up.

The available evidence

The available statistical evidence comes mainly from the ODPM's Housing Strategy Statistical Appendix (HSSA) data provided by local authorities. The overall quality of these data is a matter of concern (Crook *et al.*, forthcoming). However, the trends reflected in the data are almost certainly quite robust.

Estimates of S106 affordable housing completions show a steady increase since the turn of the century, although the overall total of affordable housing (which includes 100 per cent sites and 'purchase and repair' by housing associations) has been falling until very recently (Figure 1). These figures reflect the continuing decline in single-tenure developments across the country as the mixed-tenure mixed-communities policy takes hold (Monk *et al.*, 2005). This trend is set to continue, underlining the growing importance of S106, which now delivers over 50 per cent of all affordable units.

Figure 1 All affordable completions and S106 completions

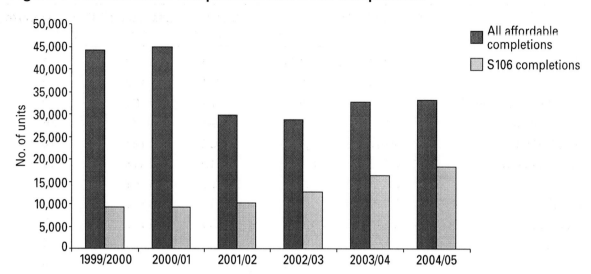

The Government's emphasis on expanding housing output overall, together with a generally benign economic environment, has been reflected in an increase in the total numbers of dwellings being completed, from under 130,000 in 2001/02 to almost 155,000 dwellings in 2004/05 (Figure 2). The proportion of affordable housing delivered through S106 agreements has risen more rapidly, so that, in 2004/05, these dwellings amounted to over 18,000 – around 12 per cent of total output. This total is heavily concentrated in London and the South (Table 1). It is also worth noting that the proportion of social rented housing is now less than two-thirds of the total and that intermediate housing is more heavily concentrated in London and the South.

Figure 2 All housing completions and S106 completions

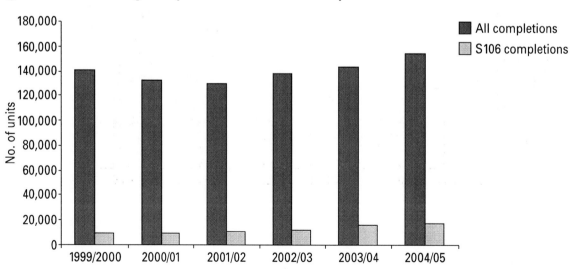

Table 1 Tenure breakdown, 2004/05

	All affordable completions	Rented	Shared ownership	Discounted sale	Other – tenure unknown
North East	186	156	30	0	0
North West	631	279	204	147	0
Yorkshire & Humberside	681	514	78	81	0
East Midlands	1,294	766	399	73	56
West Midlands	1,672	1,039	492	127	14
East of England	2,710	2,150	419	113	28
London	3,725	2,536	1,098	42	49
South East	5,327	3,122	1,916	169	49
South West	1,949	1,272	484	156	37
England	**18,175**	**11,834**	**5,120**	**908**	**233**
	100%	65%	28%	5%	1%

The evidence also shows that the number of S106 affordable units granted planning permission has risen rapidly (Figure 3). This is good news in that it suggests that the effectiveness of the S106 policy is increasing. However, it is also the case that completions are rising more slowly than permissions – which has led to concerns about the capacity of S106 and the planning system to actually deliver agreed levels of affordable housing.

Figure 3 S106 completions and permissions

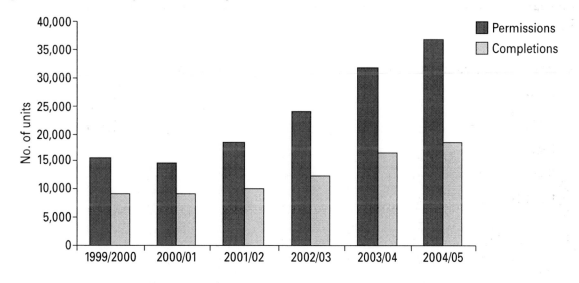

The reasons for this increasing gap between permissions and completions are unclear. One is obvious – that there is an inherent time lag between permission and completion. However, this is clearly not enough to account for the full extent of the gap. There is anecdotal evidence that points to increasing delays as well as to changes in mix and timing within developments, and lack of clarity about the use of financial instruments. These are thought to relate to: changes in the economic climate and the relevant property market; changes in ownership as development progresses; inadequately specified S106 agreements; inadequate monitoring on the part of local authorities; and incentives to developers to provide the minimum possible level of affordable housing.

In part because of the very long time lags between initial agreement and completion, little research has been undertaken to assess the delivery system in terms of either whether the project actually goes ahead or whether what is being delivered is what was originally negotiated. It is therefore timely to assess whether potential affordable homes are being lost through the renegotiation of S106 agreements or non-development of sites.

The detailed research questions

The overarching question addressed by this study is therefore 'to what extent is the affordable housing specified in the original S106 agreements actually being delivered?'. This can be broken down into four main elements.

- Has affordable housing been lost or modified through legally negotiated changes to the initial agreed S106 or because of non-take-up of a particular planning permission?

- What is the scale and extent of any change?

- Why is the change occurring?

- What patterns of behaviour are leading to change?

For example, is social rented housing sometimes converted into shared ownership, or indeed other tenures, because of a lack of funding? Are fewer units provided than were originally agreed? Are they provided in a different location or not at all? These questions raise complex issues, which include:

- the degree to which there are procedures for renegotiating the S106 agreement and the extent to which this is properly documented

- the timing of development and the extent to which the timing can be renegotiated

- in large schemes that are phased, the ordering of development, which may change – in particular, the timing of the affordable units

- the relevance of financial contributions, which may be modified, or may replace affordable units

- the mix of affordable housing that is provided, which may be different from that outlined in the S106 agreement

- the nature of the market units provided, which may be modified as compared to what was expected given the original planning permission

- the possibility that development may be postponed or may simply not go ahead.

Methods

The study involved five strands of research. The first involved a scoping study, consisting of a policy and literature review together with interviews with key actors including representatives from the Greater London Authority and London boroughs with large flagship sites where renegotiation is claimed to have taken place, regional officers from the Housing Corporation and the National Housing Federation, officers in local planning authorities (LPAs) responsible for policy and negotiations, planning consultants, English Partnerships and some of the developers themselves.

On the basis of this evidence, the second stage was to develop a typology of possible outcomes, which could be used as a framework for more detailed analysis of site-specific evidence.

The third element involved re-examining the sites that had been used in the three previous studies, which focused on the operation of S106 more generally (Crook *et al.*, 2002; Monk *et al.*, 2005; Whitehead *et al.*, 2005), to look specifically at how far the original S106 had actually been delivered on the ground. This database of sites was extended by details of other sites described by some of the respondents to the scoping study. This produced a total of 39 sites that had been completed or partly completed and where we had the necessary information about the S106 agreement.

On the basis of this secondary evidence, the local authorities, housing associations and, in some cases, the developers involved in these 39 sites were then contacted to find out whether there were any differences between the outcome and the original S106 agreement, and why these occurred.

The fourth element involved selecting six sites for more detailed study in order to explore the process whereby sites went ahead as planned or not, and to gain a better understanding of why this happened in practice. The case studies encompass sites of varying sizes and characteristics in six different local authorities, and allow a more in-depth analysis of differing experiences of S106 delivery.

A parallel study, published separately (Watson, 2006), provided a more qualitative assessment of process and outcomes with respect to affordable housing on eight sites in two local authority areas – York and Leeds. Local authorities, Registered Social Landlords (RSLs) and private developers were interviewed, and a series of round-table focus groups and site visits were held. This study aimed to provide evidence on the effectiveness of the delivery system at the local authority level as well as indicative material on whether S106 is providing high-quality affordable housing in mixed communities. Key findings from this study are used as illustrative examples in this report.

Finally, these elements have been drawn together to address the detailed questions set out above and to help understand the process by which affordable housing is being delivered – leading to conclusions and recommendations.

2 Perceptions of major stakeholders

The scoping study consisted of interviews with more than 30 representatives from the organisations listed below.

1 Public sector:
- Housing Corporation
- Greater London Authority
- National Housing Federation (NHF)
- housing associations
- local authority planners.

2 Private sector:
- the Home Builders Federation
- planning consultants
- developers.

The scoping interviews enabled a better understanding of what is happening in terms of the process of delivering new affordable housing through S106 and highlighted the main issues and concerns. The interviews, based on the perceptions of respondents, revealed a wide range of opinions about whether S106 agreements were being renegotiated and the reasons for this. The key themes arising from the interviews are explored below.

Perceptions of the effectiveness of S106 procedures

There was a range of responses about the importance of the issue. There was some feeling that 'there is a problem and it [S106] isn't delivering what was agreed, but whether the variation is great is difficult to assess', but some developers stated that they had 'no immediate sense of S106 being changed mid-stream'. The outcomes of S106 agreements are not always documented, so it is difficult to assess the scale of variation and to understand why renegotiations are taking place or how they affect the output of affordable housing, if at all.

The Housing Corporation expressed concern about whether the outputs are the same as those initially agreed and funded. NHF regional staff felt that not delivering what was originally agreed is a common occurrence and negotiations subsequent to the initial agreement can be very long and protracted with developers 'bogging down' the process. The housebuilding industry, in contrast, argued that it was rare for outputs to be changed between signing and delivery, except by request of the local authority.

A recent survey of local authorities by the ODPM (Crook *et al.*, 2006) asked local authorities whether the failure of developers to deliver planning obligations as intended was a problem for them. Only one in five authorities considered failure to deliver obligations as a problem. This question referred to all types of planning obligations. Several local authorities interviewed in our study said that they were not affected by the issue because they had dedicated and experienced teams to deal with developers where there may be 'some renegotiation around the edges' but 'no substantial renegotiation'. However, they did recognise that it was likely to be an issue for smaller local authorities, which might be inexperienced and lack negotiation skills (an issue identified in Monk *et al.*, 2005) and which may be faced with a situation 'of renegotiate or abandon the scheme'. In authorities where the S106 process worked well and where there were good relationships with developers, renegotiation did not appear to be a key concern.

Compliance with legal procedures and monitoring

There was little explicit reference among those interviewed as to whether renegotiation and deeds of variation were perceived as legal issues. Only one respondent stated that the S106 agreement cannot be changed 'because it is a signed legal agreement'. The majority of respondents felt that renegotiations were 'part and parcel' of the way developers behave. The extent of informal changes to the S106 was unclear. To some extent these practices appear to be accepted as the norm. Where there was a difference in output and a variation under S106 had not been sought, it was not generally seen as a legal issue.

Examples were cited where S106 agreements were varied by deed. One site referred to in London 'is on its third replan, each with a deed of variation', where the number of affordable units has been increased but their size has been reduced (developer interview). Similarly a site in Cardiff was cited where:

> … the developer replanned the scheme and increased the density and played around with the design. It was approved by the Planning Committee and the developer redrafted a completely new S106, which picked up what was still outstanding from the old one – it recast the payments in the light of the increased number of dwellings and the additional affordable housing.
> (Planning consultant interview)

Several respondents said that they had no feeling that developers were failing to comply with legal procedures in relation to varying or renegotiating agreements. However, others mentioned that sometimes developers might fail to comply with legal procedures because they simply 'forgot' to do so, as one respondent stated:

> I can imagine cases where something gets forgotten and, if the local authority does not remind the developer, something won't happen – but it's more likely to be financial payments rather than affordable housing. (Developer interview)

This situation where local authorities have to 'remind' developers of their obligations may be difficult where the developer is experienced and the local authority is not. There is clearly a problem of monitoring and subsequent enforcement, particularly in smaller authorities with fewer resources. One local authority experienced in dealing with S106 agreements stated that, if there was no Social Housing Grant (SHG) to fund the affordable units, there is a known cost to the RSL so that:

> ... the RSL involved monitors delivery of the contract, which specifies both the timing and the price of the units. I am 99 per cent sure that this is a watertight arrangement and that we have had no problems with it. (Planner interview)

Several respondents supported the view that formal monitoring of the outputs on all S106 schemes ought to be introduced, as this would help assess the scale of the problem (and indeed whether there really was a problem here) and may prevent non-compliance, except where changes are agreed as legitimate by all parties.

Does S106 deliver what was originally agreed?

There are mixed views among those interviewed, with some believing that S106 is not always 'delivering what was agreed', but, given the lack of monitoring, the extent and scale of variations and their legitimacy is often unknown. Respondents stated that it was not only developers who change S106 agreements but also local authorities 'where things are changed along the way for practical purposes'. Many changes are legitimate and 'sometimes circumstances can change from when the S106 was negotiated so what ends up in the development can be quite different from what was agreed by the [planning] committee'. Some examples were cited where schemes differed from those planned in the S106 agreement. For example:

> Forty-one per cent of the site was to be affordable and 25 per cent of this [for] key workers. The key worker homes were meant to be cluster units. However, over the course of the development, it was decided that cluster units were no longer viable and a change was made to the planning consent.
> (Planning consultant interview)

Where the Housing Corporation had assessed schemes, it found that details such as dwelling size might change but developments were not usually radically different. However, for schemes without SHG, the Corporation is not involved and very few local authorities and housing associations have effective monitoring systems.

An issue for the Housing Corporation can arise where a mixture of developer contribution and SHG is used. There are an enormous number of different combinations of grant and planning gain, and thus how the two sources of funds are used. The Corporation now wants to focus on the value of the grant and of the developer contribution to measure the amount of additionality. At present, it is too complicated to fully and accurately measure additionality because it requires being able to estimate whether outputs are greater on sites with SHG than on sites with planning gain alone. The Corporation has now produced an advanced development model, which can be used in negotiations to see whether the scheme maximises value for money for the public purse.

Perceived reasons for changes

In general, it was felt by respondents that renegotiations were often legitimate and in response to particular events, such as the financial viability of the scheme, subsidies that were not forthcoming and changing housing need, which shifted the demand for certain types of dwelling. However, there was anecdotal evidence that suggested that local authorities felt that, in some cases, developers were backtracking after signing the S106 agreement because it was advantageous for them to do so. A major developer said that the main reasons for change relate to changing market conditions, or at least to new evidence about market conditions. A local authority stated that, if all local authorities had 'clear policies and clarity around S106 agreements for developers', then negotiations would be straightforward and there should be no reason to change what was planned.

Most developers now use some form of cascade mechanism on large sites, which allows, for example, the provision of shared ownership rather than social rented housing. Some developers cascade all the way down to a 'trapdoor' of full-price market sale, although local authorities are now aware of the limitations of this approach, so its use is less common. The cascade mechanism means that the possibility of substituting shared ownership for social rented housing gives the developer an element of financial protection because of the lower developer subsidies involved in the provision of intermediate forms of affordable housing.

A number of respondents stated that the reasons for changes among developers were simply 'that they could get away with it'. Developers are aware that local authorities have few resources and do not want to lose sites, so it can be 'a tricky situation for the planners' who may be faced with a 'take it or leave it situation'. It was felt that the larger local authorities, and particularly those in London, appear to have 'got it cracked' in dealing with big developers and so can minimise changes and backtracking. The sharing of 'best practice' among planning authorities would help smaller, less experienced authorities to deal with developers wanting to alter S106 agreements. One important issue is the relationship between the planning and the housing departments, and how they involve housing associations in negotiation and decision making.

One of the arguments put forward by housebuilders was that, if the planning system delivers more houses in total, then it will deliver more affordable housing. They consider this preferable to trying to maximise the affordable housing component of the same total number of new homes. They argue that this worsens affordability because the same number of new market homes would have to be more expensive to cross-subsidise the extra affordable homes.

Recent research (Watson, 2006) confirmed our earlier work and found that S106 negotiations were long and complex, and at times challenging. The normal, commercial negotiating style adopted by housebuilders was seen by the local authority officers as aggressive or confrontational. Interviews with the housebuilders identified a problem in terms of loss of continuity following changes in personnel and a lack of commercial awareness on the part of some staff. This suggests a need for enhanced commercial awareness and negotiating skills among RSL and local authority staff. It was suggested that housebuilders' robust negotiating styles can include tactics such as playing RSLs off against each other to generate competition.

The scoping interviews reflected a wide range of perspectives and produced perceptions that cannot all be true, but they were useful in helping to identify the possible as well as the most likely outcomes. There is likely to be a range of potential scenarios in which the affordable housing element of an S106 agreement is not implemented as originally intended. These may depend on legal considerations or may simply be a matter of the balance of power between the developer and the planning authority. Previous research (Crook *et al.*, 2002; Monk *et al.*, 2005) showed that local authorities vary considerably in their experience and negotiation skills. Many are now highly skilled and, where this is the case, changes to the affordable housing contribution are likely to be subject to a legal change – either a deed of variation or a new S106 agreement. However, where there is less local authority expertise, often coupled with powerful developers who take advantage of this, changes may go ahead without formal legal agreement. In the extreme, a developer may simply not provide the affordable housing promised in the S106 agreement.

Thus the evidence from the interviews was that senior executives from government agencies and housing organisations were concerned about the extent to which the affordable housing agreed at the time of planning permission was actually coming forward – and especially whether it was in the form agreed. Respondents working closer to the ground on the other hand appeared much more sanguine – observing general compliance and reasons for those variations of which they were aware. The examples put forward in discussion suggested that the anecdotal evidence of significant changes and loss of affordable housing might well be overstated – perhaps because senior executives tend to get involved only when there are problems. A more general concern expressed by a minority of respondents was that they felt developers were clearly in the driving seat so they were able to modify outcomes to help themselves.

3 A framework for assessing S106 outcomes

The scoping study strongly suggested that the most usual outcome on sites that have been developed is full compliance. However, there are a range of potential scenarios in which the affordable housing element of an S106 agreement will not be implemented as originally intended. These may depend on the market; on legal considerations; or may simply be a matter of the balance of power between the developer and the planning authority.

The scoping study provided a useful starting point for developing a typology of potential outcomes (see box below). It helped to identify a range of scenarios where the affordable housing obligation of an S106 agreement might not be implemented as intended.

A typology of outcomes

1 The affordable housing element of the S106 is delivered in line with S106 and to expectations

   This will normally be the desired outcome of the S106 process – the contract is fully specified and delivered.

2 The S106 is revised and a deed of variation signed or a new S106 is negotiated and implemented

   This may be initiated by the developer, a new owner or the local authority, usually in the light of changing circumstances.

3 Post-contractual negotiation alters the output (but no deed of variation)

   All parties agree to changes in location, type, tenure, numbers and financial contribution without formally agreeing these changes.

4 The output is different from expectation but is consistent with the S106

   One or more parties did not achieve what they expected but where the relevant elements were not fully specified in the S106.

5 The planning permission is not implemented

   Either as a result of the S106 or because of other changes in circumstance.

(Continued)

6   The developer implements the permission but fails to comply with the S106 affordable housing obligation

These are situations where what was specified in the original S106 is not achieved and there is neither a deed of variation nor a post-contractual negotiation to enable change. There may also be cases where it was not clear whether the S106 was actually fully implemented because the outcome had not been monitored.

7   Outcome unknown

No data available – agreement probably delivered as agreed but outcome unknown as data cannot be verified against records.

There are seven main categories of outcome ranging from projects where the S106 had been fully delivered in line with stakeholder expectations to situations where the planning permission had not been taken up, as well as cases for which no data were available. The typology raises two types of issue – whether the formal requirements have been met and whether what has been provided meets expectations or not – for example, because the S106 was inadequately specified.

The typology describes the possible scenarios for delivering the affordable housing element, ranging from implementation as intended, through renegotiation with or without a deed of variation; to non-implementation of the planning consent. Category 6 is the only one where the S106 agreement is actually breached.

A major objective of the research is to test out this methodology and to assess whether the identified categories do indeed describe the actual outcomes. A second objective is to examine the relative importance of the different categories.

Examples from our database of sites

The first stage of our empirical research was to examine the evidence from sites for which we had adequate detail in our database to analyse the agreements and observed outcomes. This allowed us to identify examples of sites in most of the categories identified in the box above.

1   The affordable housing element of the S106 is delivered in line with S106 and to expectations

This is by far the most common outcome once development has started on sites. The appendix of case study sites lists where the affordable housing element was delivered as agreed (Appendix 1). In addition, it can be assumed that, on many of the cases where no data were obtained on delivery, the units were delivered as planned.

On the sites that are still being developed, local authorities and housing associations confirmed that the affordable housing elements were generally being built and expected that the full quota would be delivered. This is particularly the case on large sites addressed in more detail in the case study appendix (Appendix 2).

2   The S106 is revised and a deed of variation signed or a new S106 is negotiated and implemented

This situation is relatively common, especially on larger sites. It is explored in more detail in the case studies. The deed of variation may allow the local authority to increase the proportion or numbers of affordable housing actually delivered. For example, in one local authority, early S106 agreements included the negotiation of discounted market units for sale as an affordable tenure. The units were usually discounted to 80 per cent of the open market value. When these contributions were negotiated between 1998 and 2000 these units were affordable. As a consequence of the significant rise in house prices compared to incomes, such discounts now have a limited impact on affordability. The local authority renegotiated with one developer to alter the contribution when the developer pointed out that the affordable units as agreed were no longer affordable. The two parties agreed to an off-site contribution instead.

A London borough suggested that, where deeds of variation were used on S106 agreements, they often related to changes in site phasing rather than to the delivery of affordable housing as a whole. This is backed up by our research on specific sites, which found that most amendments to S106 agreements do not affect the affordable housing provision.

3   Post-contractual negotiation alters the output (but no deed of variation)

This situation might arise where all relevant parties accept changes in location, type, tenure, numbers, or financial contribution without formally agreeing these changes. This is relatively uncommon, as parties tend to have a preference for ensuring that the agreement is official. However, one case was mentioned where additional Social Housing Grant became available once the houses had been completed and ownership had been transferred by the developer to the housing association, and the local authority and housing association decided to offer the units for social rented rather than intermediate housing.

4   The output is different from expectation but is consistent with the S106

This situation can occur where one or more parties did not achieve what they expected, but the relevant elements were not fully specified in the S106. For example, it was noted by one respondent that they were disappointed with the quality of the units provided. Private development of market housing may not always meet Housing Corporation space or lifetime homes standards, for example. However, this problem is related to the quality of new housing overall, rather than of affordable housing alone.

The target for affordable housing provision is now 50 per cent in York and in defined areas of Leeds. In these areas, the supply of sites being brought forward for development has declined or stopped. Research in York and Leeds (Watson, 2006) found that some RSL and local authority representatives were concerned about the impact of high affordable housing targets (up to 50 per cent), which were seen as producing higher densities, smaller dwellings and a general intensification of development, as well as a decline in the numbers of sites being brought forward for development. RSLs may also feel that they cannot push too hard in a competitive environment between RSLs, so some may limit negotiation with developers to price and mix.

5   The planning permission is not implemented

Local authorities estimate that, on average, approximately 80 per cent of full planning permissions (75 per cent for outline permissions) are implemented (Crook *et al.*, 2006). This is difficult to assess in that a five-year delay (now three years) must expire before it can be stated with any certainty that the planning permission has expired and the units will not be built. Evidence from local authorities suggests that this situation is very rare in highly pressured areas, so that differences between permission given and completions are largely accounted for by delays. However, a London borough stated that, in some cases, a developer may apply for permission to help gauge the value of a site, but that new planning permission is applied for later on. In such cases, there may be double counting of affordable units, as permission for the provision of housing on the site has been given twice.

6   The developer implements the permission but fails to comply with the S106 affordable housing obligation

This is extremely rare – despite the anecdotes from the scoping study, no evidence of this was found in our database. As noted above, only one in five authorities considers failure on the part of developers to deliver obligations (including affordable housing provision) as a problem.

7   Outcome unknown

This case was relatively common. Problems in retrieving data included: multiple names for each site; several sites to which information might have applied; staff turnover since negotiations and completions; poor record keeping; and record misplacement. It is clear that better monitoring would reduce the number of cases where the outcome cannot be ascertained.

Summary of evidence

Overall, the evidence suggests that implementing S106 affordable housing agreements is by no means straightforward, with different and changing stakeholders operating in ways that were not always envisaged when the original agreement was made. The number of cases where no data were available was also concerning, suggesting that post-permission monitoring is often quite limited. Even so, the most usual outcome where development had been completed was that the affordable housing had been provided as specified.

4 The process of implementation: the evidence

The next stage was to look in more depth at the processes by which permissions are turned into completions and the factors that modify outcomes. This analysis employed three types of information: statistical evidence on the relationship between permissions and completions; the collection of additional information from stakeholders involved in the database sites; and six detailed case studies of sites, plotting expected and actual outcomes. The objective was to exemplify the relationship between what is found on the ground and our typology, and to set out lessons that can be learned for the future.

We examined our database of sites, approaching as many of the individual site stakeholders involved as possible, in order to establish whether the number of units delivered matched the number and type agreed. Additional interviews with local authority and RSL staff provided further evidence to aid our analysis. These raised some general issues about when and why completions were not occurring as well as site-specific evidence.

General issues

1 Non-take-up of planning permissions

Whether a specific permission will be built out is extremely difficult to assess. Planning permissions are valid for a period of at least five years from their date of consent (three years since 2004). Some large schemes may be completed over a decade after the original permission. Further, it is quite possible that sites with lapsed permissions may be developed at a future date.

Affordable housing completions are between 50 and 63 per cent of permissions for 1999/00–2004/05. If 25 per cent of permissions are not implemented and there is some double counting because new permissions are substituted for old and are not identified as such, this still leaves a substantial shortfall in the number of completions, even allowing for a reasonable development lag. This shortfall is made up of cases where the number of completed units is below the number agreed in the permission or where the lag between permission and completion is greater than assumed. This research identified a small number of cases where what was delivered did not match what was agreed and many more where the site was not yet completely built out. It would require much better monitoring of completions to put an accurate estimate of the number of units lost in this manner.

Why do developers fail to implement permissions? They may apply for planning permission to gauge the value of a site before selling it on, rather than because they intend to develop it. Anecdotal evidence suggests that they may be able to make more money by trading land than by the development and sale of units. A speculative planning application is inexpensive when compared to the potential gains in value. Speculative applications are common in a rising market and, where these are approved, this increases the number of permissions compared to the number of completions. Set against this are the resources involved in negotiating an S106, which may well be significant enough to reduce the number of speculative applications on large, complex sites.

In some instances, developers may purchase options to buy land from landowners, at some future date. In such cases, speculative planning permissions may be sought by a developer who does not own the land for which an outline permission is sought. This mechanism allows developers to limit their financial outlay, while securing land for future development.

This lack of implementation has implications for local plans, as it makes it difficult to accurately predict site development over the short term (12 months) and medium term (five years). It does not suggest that sites should be over-allocated, however, since developer behaviour may favour non-development of a site for a variety of reasons, not linked to S106 requirements or planning restrictions.

2 Delays in site development

The second main reason for agreed permissions not matching take-ups is the time it takes to build out the agreed development, especially on large sites. There may be delays before development starts because of resource constraints. Further, the complexities of large building projects can lead to long and variable time lags during development. Phasing and the complexities of project finance also add to delays, since the developer is likely to have to forward fund any affordable units, so will need to make sure there is sufficient revenue generated from the market units to fund the affordable units. Depending on the phasing of affordable housing provision, this may mean delays of over ten years between permission and completion.

The statistical evidence presented in Chapter 1 suggests that the extent of these delays may have remained quite stable, even though totals have increased since the turn of the century. For instance, if a lag of two years is assumed, completions vary from around two-thirds to almost 90 per cent of permissions over the years from 2000/01 to 2004/05. The pattern is not consistent but, if anything, suggests that development is being speeded up. However, because planning permissions have increased rapidly this century, we have yet to see the benefits. What is clear is that the larger the site the longer to completion – but this is not a function of the affordable housing policy, rather a feature of the private development process and an outcome of the shift from 100 per cent social housing sites to mixed-tenure schemes.

3 Double counting of units given planning permission

There is a possibility of double counting of units given planning permission, which helps explain the difference between permissions and completions. This can happen if an existing planning permission is superseded by a new permission (consisting of a new planning agreement). For example, a developer receives planning permission in 1998 for 1,000 market units and 250 affordable units. The developer does not implement the permission. The developer sells the site to a new developer who then submits a new application for 1,200 market units and negotiates a new S106 agreement, which includes 300 affordable dwellings. The affordable dwellings are eventually completed in early 2006. The 1998 HIP data (Housing Strategy Statistical Appendix) records the 250 affordable units agreed. The 2003 HIP data records 300 affordable dwellings agreed. There has been double counting of the number of units agreed on the site. The 300 units are eventually recorded as completed in 2006. Completions are clearly a more accurate reflection of the delivery of affordable units, although the number of units agreed does provide a good indication of trends.

4 Discrepancies in definitions

There are also possible explanations for discrepancies in the figures relating to the definitions of affordable housing employed. Our database included several sites where the affordable houses were actually market housing with 'restricted floorspace' (referred to as low-cost market housing), or available for discounted sale or student housing. This type of affordable housing was considered acceptable and affordable in the early years of the policy even though it does not require any RSL involvement (Policy Planning Statement 3 removes low-cost market housing from the definition of affordable housing). It is possible that some local authorities will not record the units as new affordable housing on Housing Strategy Statistical Appendix (HSSA) returns without RSL involvement in the units. Again, there is considerable room for interpretation and therefore inconsistencies in the data.

Some of the reasons listed above apply mainly to sites that have not yet been or will never be developed as anticipated in the original planning agreements. The next section uses the database of sites and case study information to consider what happens on sites that have been or are being developed.

Site-specific findings

An important element of the research programme was to examine sites where development had taken place. This was achieved via the analysis of the database of sites developed as part of previous studies as well as additional sites suggested by scoping study respondents. This concentrated on a total of 39 sites with known S106 agreements signed between 1998 and 2005, which had been completed or partly completed. The local authorities, housing associations and in some cases the developers involved in these sites were then contacted to establish whether there were any differences between the outcome and the original S106 agreement, and why these had occurred. Details of the sites are presented in Appendix 1.

The database developed from previous research contained a wide variety of sites from the very small (building just three affordable units) to the very large (building over 700 affordable units in the first phase alone) spread around England. There had been no breaches of S106 agreements relating to affordable housing.

Of the 39 developments from the original dataset, in ten cases the RSL or the local authority were either uncontactable or unable to identify the site from their records. Many attempts were made to contact local authorities and housing associations and ask them to access their records, yet some seemed to be unable to access official records that would tell them whether or not the S106 agreement was in fact delivered. This itself is of concern, as it suggests there may be serious difficulties in some local authorities in monitoring the completion of S106 agreements.

Of the 29 sites for which information was available, 24 had all been developed as originally agreed. On these 24 sites the only variations to S106 agreements related to non-housing matters and there were no other changes in terms of the numbers or sizes of units produced. One RSL commented, however, that the standard of the social rented houses built was not as high as they had expected.

On five sites, despite the planning permission being granted prior to 2000, at the end of 2005 the sites were still being developed. These five sites together account for 578 out of the 2,174 affordable units for which planning permission had been granted, meaning that 27 per cent of units granted planning permission prior to 2000 were on sites that were still incomplete at the end of 2005 and may not yet have been built.

This suggests that, although long delays between permissions and completions may occur only in a small number of sites, they are often on the very large sites producing a high proportion of the total number of affordable housing units, and so may have a disproportionate impact on the time lag between the granting of planning permission and completion.

In the cases examined, where commuted sums were agreed, or where an RSL bought land on the open market and acted as the developer, no problems were encountered.

Examples of S106 implementation

In addition to the above list of sites, this and previous research has uncovered many examples of the process by which S106 sites come to be built and many cases where there may be changes to the original agreement. However, in all these cases, there was no breach of the S106 agreement relating to affordable housing provision. Some examples are outlined below.

Example 1 Large site delivered as agreed

This is a large development with permission for almost 2,000 homes. The development is phased, with the S106 agreement divided between the six developers working there. At least four housing associations are also involved. The developer working with one association has three different elements of the site. From the association's point of view it is difficult to tell whether the S106 agreement is delivering the overall total of affordable housing that was originally agreed – their affordable housing is only a fraction of a much larger site. But, on their fraction, the developer has delivered as originally agreed. The housing association commented that, where the developers have had to renegotiate with a local authority, it has always been over the phasing or other non-housing matters:

We have found that they always deliver the agreed S106.

Example 2 Small site delivered as agreed

A former football ground is an example of a small site that delivered the agreed 33 dwellings of which ten were affordable (30 per cent). The S106 was checked by the council's legal department and it had been met as originally set out. Monitoring by the legal department makes it much easier to check compliance. The planning permission had minor changes but these were related to relocating the access to the football ground and the erection of walls and gates, not to the S106 agreement.

Example 3 Renegotiation of minor details within the S106

This is an example where there were some minor renegotiations of the S106 but not the affordable housing element. The total number of dwellings agreed was 385 of which 97 were affordable, which is 25 per cent (in line with the plan policy). Of the affordable units, 70 were for rent with the aid of SHG, while 27 were shared ownership, which did not require grant. The two types of tenure were built in separate blocks of flats, but close to one another. The affordable housing was totally separate from the market housing, which was on a different level:

> Effectively there was a party wall between the two types of housing, almost making it two different sites.

In terms of mix of dwelling sizes, there were 75 affordable two-bed flats, 13 three-bed flats and nine one-bed flats. A housing association was brought into the negotiations after the initial discussions but before the S106 was signed. The developer delivered the affordable housing as originally agreed, along with the market housing. However, there was some renegotiation – over the type of public art that was to be provided as part of the S106. They got an agreement to provide a mural instead of a statue. This did not affect the housing in any way.

These examples suggest that most renegotiation is not over affordable housing but other minor details within the S106, such as the artwork in example 3. It is quite common to renegotiate planning permission, but not over the affordable housing. Another change might be in the level of the commuted sum payable – *One London borough typically index-links commuted sums so that the final sum payable increases as market conditions become more favourable to the developer.* This is an effective way of ensuring that maximum value is obtained when site development takes several years to come forward after planning permission is given. However, this does not require a change to the S106, but is rather included in the S106 from the outset.

There are some exceptions to this – one case concerned differences in the *quality* of the affordable dwellings as defined by the Housing Corporation. In this instance, the original S106 specified land for six two-bed units to be transferred at nil value to the RSL. This density was in line with that of the three-bed market housing on the rest of the site. However, Housing Corporation space standards meant that the land could accommodate only five two-bed affordable units, so at a very late stage the local authority agreed to lose one unit. Research in York and Leeds found that differences in standards between the market and affordable housing within a scheme seemed to vary on a scheme-by-scheme basis, and depended on the housebuilder involved. Similarly, there was no consistency of approach in relation to specification. In most schemes, specification and fittings tended to be different rather than inferior, in order to meet RSL maintenance preferences. However, one housebuilder appeared to be 'playing the game', by omitting standard items from the market-value properties in their offer to the RSLs, where they knew that those elements were of value to the RSL: an example is the provision of showers. The RSL then had to pay extra to reintroduce them (Watson, 2006).

Another exception is where the *tenure* of the dwellings changes. One example is where the affordable housing was intended as shared ownership but at the last minute the Housing Corporation was able to provide SHG, which converted the dwellings to social rented units. Another is where social rented units were agreed in the S106 agreement but no SHG was available so they became shared ownership, which did not require grant to make them viable. Because the units had already been transferred to the housing association, the developer was not involved in the change of tenure.

There are particular issues with *large sites*. Large sites are more complicated so developers may want to renegotiate as external factors change – market demand, site conditions and finances, for example. Owners of large sites are also more likely to trade parcels to other developers – or even sell the whole site – and the new owners may want to renegotiate. However, even on large sites, the new owners do not always renegotiate but may deliver what was originally agreed.

Example 4 Complex large site

This hospital site is a good example of a complex large site. The site was bought by the developer who specialises in the redevelopment of brownfield land. The development was in phases, and the first phase was originally for 400 units, of which 21 were affordable, 11 social rented and ten low-cost home

(Continued)

ownership. Phase 1 on its own went very well and delivered all that was originally agreed. It is popular with residents, both on the sale side and the rented side. However, after the first phase was complete, to cut risk, the developer packaged the site into parcels, which were sold on to other developers. As a result the development has not progressed as quickly as originally planned. The housing association has now become involved with multiple developers who inherited the S106 agreement. The association also bought one parcel, which they have developed themselves. The affordable housing is spread throughout the site, although it is described as 'chunk pepper potting, because there were three different phases to it, but it is not all shoved in one corner' according to the housing association. The site is now in its third and final phase, which is being progressed as a demonstration project for the Urban Village Task Force. The housing association is the only one on the site, taking over the S106 affordable housing as well as its own development, and the main difference is that its own development is of a better standard. The developers have all met their S106 obligations in terms of the numbers, but they did not produce dwellings of the same standard as those built by the housing association.

It is important to distinguish between failures to deliver that relate to S106 and those that relate to delays that are endemic in the system, particularly for large sites. In one example all is being delivered in full according to the S106 agreement but the timescale has been drawn out, taking longer to fulfil the requirements of S106. It will be another year before the last phase is completed, yet work started in 1999.

It is also important to note that examples of lack of delivery, other than those due to non-implementation or delay, are quite rare. However, such cases may be more common in areas with the poorest monitoring and, as such, it is difficult to gauge the scale of this problem with accuracy.

Findings from six case studies

Six case studies were selected to provide a wide range of examples of different S106 developments, in terms of locations, sizes, densities and levels of success in delivering affordable housing. In several cases the S106 agreements were renegotiated as circumstances changed. Each case represents a distinct example of the ways in which S106 agreements are affected by changing circumstances within developments. The six cases are outlined in Appendix 2.

Case 1 is a mid-sized development on a brownfield site in the East of England. The original (1999) planning agreement included market housing, affordable flats, student accommodation, a fire station, and a range of community and commercial facilities. The original S106 agreement specified the provision of commuted sums for landscaping, road provision and a new fire station, as well as 40 affordable flats. The fire station provision was replaced by a payment of £120,000, and commuted sums paid in lieu of landscaping and community facility provision, while £1,765,920 was paid in lieu of affordable housing because of the high anticipated service costs for the integrated affordable units. The planning department stated that, in future, the viability of their affordable elements would be ascertained before permission is given. In terms of our typology of sites, this case fits both type 2 (the S106 is revised and a deed of variation signed or a new S106 is negotiated and implemented) and type 4 (the output is different from expectation but is consistent with the [revised] S106).

Case study 2 focuses on a complex development in London. An extremely large and complicated site, it provides an insight into the difficulties and advantages of using S106 agreements. Outline planning permission was granted for a mixed-use development in 1998. The S106 agreement (signed in 2002) committed the developer to providing a comprehensive package of affordable housing, transport links and improvements, highways works, education and community contributions, and open space provision. Phase 1 (1,065 dwellings, of which 515 affordable) of the development is now complete. A developer application (2002) to increase the number of residential units was refused by the local authority and at appeal in 2003. The local authority recently renegotiated the outline planning permission in an attempt to attain a higher number of affordable units, but this was unsuccessful. Changing market circumstances and a desire that the affordable contribution should reflect changes in need do not mean that the local authority can force renegotiation of an S106 agreement. This illustrates how a well-written and well-organised planning agreement can ensure a level of certainty for all parties, even on large and complicated developments. This example fits type 1 in our typology (the affordable housing element of the S106 is delivered in line with S106 and to expectations).

Two former hospital sites in London (534 dwellings and 385 dwellings respectively) were reviewed in case studies 3 and 4. These two large regeneration sites in London represent examples of the complexities of large phased sites. In both cases the local authority had clear guidelines and specifications for affordable housing provision set out in their local plan, and the planning departments always received support from their local councillors for a tough negotiating stance on affordable housing issues. At the outline planning approval stage the affordable housing commitments were 20 per cent (case study 3) and 25 per cent (case study 4), as well as contributions for schools, transport and community facilities. In both cases the developers wished to increase the size of the development and renegotiate their planning permissions and S106 commitments. In both instances an increase in the number of dwelling units led to a commensurate increase in the number of affordable units provided. In case 3, higher percentage requirements regarding affordable housing in the local plan meant that an increase in the percentage of affordable housing on the additional units added to the development was achieved – resulting in 22 per cent affordable housing in the development overall (up from an original 20 per cent). In case 4 the affordable housing element remained at 25 per cent, in line with the local plan requirement, despite a challenge by the Greater London Authority to increase this. These two cases are examples of type 3 of our typology (the S106 is revised and a deed of variation signed or a new S106 is negotiated and implemented).

Case 5 is a large greenfield site in the South West, part of a development area allocated in the 1999 local plan. From an affordable housing perspective this development represents a missed opportunity. A single development consortium negotiated an outline planning permission for around 5,500 dwellings on the site in 1992 (without an S106). A further outline permission was applied for and granted in 1998, as the 1992 one had lapsed. The 1998 S106 agreement required developer contributions for infrastructure and the provision of 440 affordable dwellings (8 per cent of the total). SHG was provided. The affordable units are in pockets of 40–50 units around the site, providing limited integration. When questioned about the quality of the new housing developments, the local Mayor responded:

> I had a look at the … building and I thought it was quite a nice construction. It looked quite modern and it had some shape to it.
> (BBC Wiltshire, 5 January 2006)

This is an example of type 1 in our typology (the affordable housing element of the S106 is delivered in line with the S106 and to expectations).

Case 6 is a predominantly rural development at a former barracks in the South East, where the original S106 agreement was adhered to and is now almost complete. It has been used as an 'exemplar' case by those involved and has been on the finalist list for the Deputy Prime Minister's Sustainable Community Awards. Planning permission for 348 dwellings, a large proportion of the total housing allocation for the district, was given for the 57-acre site in 1999. Development was phased between 1999 and 2006. The scheme was designed on 'urban village' principles, with a 'pepper-potted' mix of tenures and uses, with early involvement of the local community. The S106 agreement specified the provision of 96 affordable units and commuted sums for community, education and transport facilities. Social Housing Grant was made available for the affordable units at 100 per cent Total Cost Indicator net of on-costs. The development includes a range of business and commercial services as well as health and leisure facilities, a day nursery, housing, a community farm, bus service and a nursing home. This is also an example of type 1 of the typology (the affordable housing element of the S106 is delivered in line with the S106 and to expectations).

The cases provide examples of some of the possibilities when S106 agreements are used to deliver affordable housing. Density and quality tend to reflect the density and quality of the overall developments, and there is little evidence of high levels of segregation between market and affordable units in the cases examined here. In addition, the cases highlight the competing demands on S106 agreements, where funding is sought not only for affordable housing but also for the provision of community facilities and contributions towards infrastructure development.

Table 2 provides an overview of the case studies examined. It should be remembered that the case studies were chosen to give examples of different outcomes, not to reflect the relative importance of these different outcomes.

The overall conclusion from this section of the research, which has looked in greater detail at particular sites is that most of the schemes that actually get built do so as originally agreed and that, in general, the S106 delivers the planned number of affordable housing units. The problems observed relate mainly to the complexities of large sites and to changes in ownership and economic conditions.

Table 2 The six case studies

Case	Total size	Affordable in original S106 (%)	Affordable delivered or being delivered (%)	Commuted sum instead of affordable?	S106 change?	SHG?	Level of integration	Affordable % in local plan at time of outline permission?	Year of outline planning permission	What happened?
1	157 flats, 300 student rooms and 2 warden flats	30	0	Yes – £1,765,920	Yes – affordable housing changed to commuted sum	No	Full integration	30%	1999	Not affordable, because of linked service costs
2	1,065 in Phase 1 of which 515 affordable	50	50	No	Not to affordable element	Some	High levels of integration	50% London requirement	1998	Affordable delivered as intended
3	534, increased from 442	20	22	No	Yes – increase in affordable	No	High levels of integration	20%	2003 (but 1996 for whole site)	More affordable because of increase in development size
4	385, increased from 341	25	25	No	Yes – increase in affordable	No	Pepper potting of affordable units	25%	2002	More affordable because of increase in development size
5	5,500	8	8	No	Original outline permission in 1992 had no affordable	Yes	Affordable in pockets of 40–50 units around the site	No set level. No set level in new deposit plan	1998	S106 obligations met, *but* poor levels of delivery, poor design of scheme
6	348	28	28	No	No – scheme went ahead as agreed	Yes	Full integration	No set level	1999	S106 obligations met. Highly rated development

5 The main messages: conclusions and implications

On the evidence presented here, once development starts on a site, S106 delivers what was originally agreed in the majority of cases. The most important explanation for the disparity between planning permissions and completions is that either schemes were not developed or there were very long delays between permission and completion. Larger sites tend to be the most affected, not because of anything in the S106 agreement or affordable housing requirements, but because of the financial and logistical complexities of developing large sites. The larger scale also means that there is often inter-trading of smaller parcels of land between developers, which may delay development and result in the need for renegotiation of S106 agreements.

Conclusions

Large sites

A particularly important aspect associated with large sites is the phasing of development. A reasonable marketing strategy implies that the whole site should not be built out in one go. In this context some sites take so long to develop that the market has changed and, if the developer cannot sell the market-price houses, then the affordable housing cannot be delivered. Many S106 agreements, for instance, now include a clause whereby it is the actual occupation of the market housing that triggers the delivery of affordable housing. Others allow for changes in tenure. Off-site provision of affordable units can also be difficult to deliver to the main site development timescale.

The main reason why affordable housing completions are so much lower than the figures for permissions granted is therefore not related to the S106 as such but to the complexities of development, particularly on brownfield sites. It is an important aspect of the shift towards mixed-tenure development in that 100 per cent sites could be built in a single phase. Linking affordable housing directly to market development therefore inherently slows down the process of achieving the required output.

Renegotiation

S106 agreements are renegotiated but not often with respect to the affordable housing element. Where renegotiation does occur it can sometimes deliver more dwellings – for example, where the original planning permission is renegotiated to provide a larger total number of units. In these circumstances the numbers of affordable units may also increase. Such renegotiation is not strictly the outcome of the S106 agreement – in these examples, the outcome was more affordable housing through increased market unit densities, rather than because a higher proportion of affordable housing was negotiated.

This raises an interesting question about the wording of the S106 agreement. If it specifies a number of dwellings, and densities change, the local authority can lose out (relative to what it might have achieved), whereas if it specifies a percentage of the market dwellings, then both parties benefit from increasing densities.

Another issue that particularly affects large sites is the extent to which planning permission is renegotiated in cases where the local plan has been reviewed since the original permission was given. This has usually meant that a larger proportion of affordable housing is now required.

Are aspirations consistent with outcomes?

There is considerable evidence that some earlier S106 agreements were inadequately detailed and as a result, although agreements have not been breached, affordable housing outcomes have not been as good as expected.

It is clear from our discussions that planners, the planning system and other local authority and housing association staff are becoming more sophisticated with regard to such negotiations. Watson's (2006) related research found that earlier schemes generated significantly fewer dwellings than the target (which were not founded in clear policy or housing demand studies), but, as policies became more sophisticated and the housing needs justification more robust, there was less argument (and thus change). The increasing skills and knowledge of professionals in using and responding to the new planning environment are also likely to tighten up future S106 agreements. What remains unclear is how effective the monitoring process is after the agreement has been put in place.

Local authorities are at very different positions in terms of development of policy and practice, and those interviewed were quite clear on the value of sharing experience between local authorities and publication of good-practice guidance. The overriding conclusion is that all parties want certainty so that they can negotiate more effectively and reduce their risks accordingly.

Complexity

Although there is evidence of increasing understanding, one of the most important findings of this and earlier research is that situations on the ground are far more complicated than a simple market conditions model could predict. This is because of a number of factors.

- When negotiating an S106 a developer may predict profits on a development scheduled to commence at a point five years or more into the future.

- The planning authority on the other hand usually appears to be negotiating a deal based on land and property values at the time of the negotiation.

- If the housing market falls, the developer is in a position to renegotiate the planning permission (and S106) at a future date. Moreover, index-linking S106 commitments to market conditions does not prevent a developer reapplying for planning permission (with new S106 commitments) if the market falls.

- The true cost of the affordable housing element will link to quantity, quality, size, layout, level of integration, type of tenure, size and type of overall development, other S106 commitments and other planning conditions – it is therefore extremely difficult to predict and may generate very different outcomes from those envisaged. For instance, Watson (2006) found that, where space standards are below the Housing Corporation's Scheme Development Standards (SDS), the general policy of RSLs is to under-let, so that, for example, a three-bedroom five-person house would be let to a four-person household, which disguises inferior value for money.

Value for money

This is an important issue with respect to what is negotiated. RSLs see planning gain deals as a means to increase supply of affordable housing, above that which they can achieve through the Housing Corporation's National Affordable Housing Programme (NAHP) funding (this is the new name for what used to be termed the Approved Development Programme or ADP funding). An analysis of the value for money of eight sites in York and Leeds generated some interesting but somewhat contradictory results (Watson, 2006). All of the schemes were 'off-the-shelf' purchases of completed dwellings without SHG. All these prices were below the Housing Corporation's Total Cost Indicator (TCI), but some of them were surprisingly high, bearing in mind no SHG was provided. On the other hand, the percentages of open-market vacant-possession value for which the affordable units were acquired are low. In the majority of cases, the price was below the likely build cost of the dwellings, as a result of which the contribution to land value was either modest or negative. This demonstrates that the use of planning gain is generating 'cross-subsidy' – whether this derives from reduced profit margins to housebuilders or reduced site valuations for the vendors is unclear.

These findings are consistent with our earlier research across a wider range of sites and areas, which showed that contributions were often only enough to bring costs below Total Cost Indicators and so make the development eligible for subsidy. It also showed that RSLs often made considerable contributions from their own resources and that, while landowners and developers felt they were paying quite heavily, the actual contributions often accounted for only a relatively small proportion of development value (Monk *et al.*, 2005).

Implications

If a significant proportion of sites are not going to be developed how should this affect the planning process, particularly with respect to the operation of the local development framework? If planners know from experience that some sites will not come forward, do they over-allocate in order to ensure they will reach their housing targets? If so, does this mean the affordable housing element is also over-allocated? This has implications for funding, particularly if SHG has been allocated to units that are not built out, as well as for the delivery of affordable housing. The grant may be allocated to other schemes to enable the provision of social rented rather than intermediate housing, for example.

The reverse can also happen if Social Housing Grant is not allocated for planned social rented units, which are then built as shared ownership or fewer numbers of social rented units. The Housing Corporation has made it a matter of principle not to use SHG on S106 sites *except* in special circumstance. However, both this study and earlier research (Monk *et al.*, 2005) suggest that the use of SHG is essential in some areas to ensure viability (for example on brownfield sites in London), so there will undoubtedly have to be exceptions. In London, for instance, the HSSA data show that the number of affordable units produced on S106 sites without grant halved between 2003/04 and 2005/06.

Another implication of our findings is the importance of the economic environment. In particular, the cases examined have generally been developed in a booming housing market, with rising dwelling values. Sites have often been completed a number of years after the S106 planning agreements have been signed. In a rising market this means that the impact of the original S106 agreement on a developer's profit margin is reduced – and it is therefore easier for the developer to deliver their S106 commitments. Hence, it appears that everyone benefits. The dependence on the market is critical, as developers tend to rely on rising markets to help meet obligations. Of course, if the housing market fell, the developer would find it much more difficult to deliver affordable housing than might have originally been anticipated. The introduction of index-linking may well represent a new approach to ensuring that changing market conditions are increasingly factored into S106 agreements.

In this context, there is some evidence that housebuilders who are not familiar with local policies may have over-bid for sites if they do not factor the costs of affordable housing planning gain deals into their offers prior to acquisition of the site (Crook *et al.*, 2002; Watson, 2006). This issue has been less important to developers because of the increases in sales values during the development periods of most of the sample schemes, but this could change.

Monitoring delivery

In many case studies the local authority and RSL staff were unable to answer the question of how many units had been delivered on a site and whether this was consistent with the S106 agreement. There are few systems in place that actually record the details of the S106 and then monitor with reference to the original agreement. It would be very easy to implement a monitoring system within local authorities whereby the contents of an S106 were clearly accessible so all parties could check compliance. Indeed, the new Planning Policy Statement 3 does take steps to improve the monitoring of planning obligations.

An alternative method of monitoring is to use the RSLs to check that what is being delivered to them matches the planning agreement. The problem is that many RSLs are not involved in the S106 negotiations and are not familiar with the contents of the agreement. An improved monitoring system would make it easier for local authorities and RSLs to complete the appropriate statistical returns. This would improve the quality of the data available for analysis.

The poor monitoring of planning agreements makes it very difficult to gather data on specific sites. Staff turnover in local authorities and RSLs is high and, when staff are questioned over a specific site that was granted planning permission five years ago, many of them are unfamiliar with it and cannot provide details, as the files are now inaccessible. Improved monitoring would allow us to draw a much clearer picture on the failure of developers to deliver affordable housing.

What is being delivered

The evidence presented here suggests that, at least in a stable economic environment, S106 is being implemented effectively. But it also points to some major issues that have yet to be addressed. The first is simply that, as S106 becomes more and more dominant as the means for achieving mixed-tenure and affordable housing, the capacity to increase output has declined because of the loss of non-S106 sites (Crook *et al.*, 2002; Monk *et al.*, 2005). Even if all sites above threshold delivered 25 per cent this would still leave a massive shortfall in the additional affordable housing required.

Second, the shift away from social rented housing associated both with the lower public cost of providing intermediate-tenure housing and with the mixed-communities policy has important implications for meeting the need for adequate accommodation for all. Social rented housing now accounts for less than two-thirds of S106 output and even less in the most pressured areas of London and the South East. This shift in provision has further implications in terms of the type of dwelling being provided as well as the quality and cost of that output.

Third, there is increasing evidence of a tension between increasing the output of affordable housing through the planning system with the help of public subsidy and forcing development without that subsidy. An apparently obvious way forward here is to determine contributions by a financial formula – but the complexity of sites and circumstances suggests that this is unlikely to be more effective except in the most straightforward conditions.

Summary of findings

- In the vast majority of cases, once the development process gets under way, the S106 agreements are implemented in full.

- There is a slower pace of implementation on the largest sites but this is not because of the affordable housing agreement. In particular, there is much renegotiation of the details of original planning consents, not least because developers often 'break up' the development site by selling on parts to other developers who then seek to renegotiate the original consent to extract more development value.

- Output from S106 depends therefore on (a) the flow of land through the planning system and (b) the state of demand for private housing developments. Tinkering with the details of S106 affordable housing policy is much less important as a means of maximising output than ensuring that land is available to the private sector and that households want to buy homes from them.

- Where S106 agreements do not get implemented it is usually because the development of the site as a whole does not go ahead and for reasons unrelated to the S106.

- S106 agreements need to be better specified. In many cases expertise has been developed since the agreements considered in this report were drawn up, leading to a qualitative improvement in the content of more recent S106 agreements.

- Monitoring is poorly developed and, given the growing importance of S106 to the delivery of affordable housing, it is important that both LPAs and RSLs develop better monitoring systems drawing on the good practice in place in some authorities.

The current system works reasonably well and is largely accepted. It is not without problems but these can be addressed. Improving what has become accepted practice could have a greater chance of working than the more radical changes proposed by the Government, such as a Planning Gain Supplement (PGS). The S106 approach is providing land and this land is more likely than in the past to be in the right places to meet the mixed communities and the increasingly market-oriented agendas. Equally, the approach helps to enable a range of tenures within the affordable housing sector.

However, problems remain. The system for providing affordable housing is becoming increasingly dependent on the buoyancy of the private housing market. If the market falters so will the provision of affordable housing. Moreover, the provision of affordable housing is still heavily dependent on public funding – and it will therefore be extremely difficult to expand provision in the way envisaged in government policy statements without more government money.

Overall, the answer to our research question is clear. The implementation stage seems to be working pretty well in its own terms – but this is only a necessary condition for success. There are many other fundamental issues that remain to be addressed.

References

Barker, K. (2004) *Review of Housing Supply: Interim Report.* London: HM Treasury

Crook, A., Currie, J., Jackson, A., Monk, S., Rowley, S., Smith, K. and Whitehead, C. (2002) *Planning Gain and Affordable Housing: Making it Count.* York: York Publishing Services/Joseph Rowntree Foundation

Crook, A.D.H., Henneberry, J.M., Rowley, S., Tait, M. and Watkins, C. with the Halcrow Group (2006) *Valuing Planning Obligations in England.* London: ODPM

Crook, A.D.H., Monk, S.M., Rowley, S. and Whitehead, C.M.E. (forthcoming) 'Planning gain and the supply of affordable housing in England: understanding the numbers', *Town Planning Review*

DETR (1998) *Circular 06/98: Affordable Housing.* London: DETR

Monk, S., Crook, T., Lister, D., Rowley, S., Short, C. and Whitehead, C. (2005) *Land and Finance for Affordable Housing: The Complementary Roles of Social Housing Grant and the Provision of Affordable Housing through the Planning System.* York: Joseph Rowntree Foundation

ODPM (2005a) *Update to PPG3: Housing: Planning for Sustainable Communities in Rural Areas.* London: ODPM

ODPM (2005b) *Update to PPG3: Housing: Supporting the Delivery of New Housing.* London: ODPM

Watson, J. (2006) *Understanding Planning Gain: What Works?* York: Joseph Rowntree Foundation, York

Whitehead, C., Monk, S., Lister, D. and Short, C. with Crook, T., Henneberry, J. and Rowley, S. (2005) *The Value for Money of Delivering Affordable Housing through Section 106.* London: ODPM

Appendix 1: The sites

Site number	Region	% affordable	Total number of units	Number of affordable units	Affordable housing element of S106
1	London	25	385	97	Delivered as agreed
2	London	24	204	49	No data
3	London		169	Commuted sum	Commuted sum of £2,468,389 paid
4	North East	5	560	30	Under construction
5	North East	10	600	60	Under construction
6	North East	10	250	26	Delivered as agreed
7	East Midlands	28	425	120	Under construction
8	East Midlands	25	277	70	Delivered as agreed
9	East Midlands	3	40	1	Delivered as agreed
10	East Midlands	22	137	30	Delivered as agreed
11	South East	7	41	3	Site completed, no data
12	London	31	1,665	515	Under construction
13	London	100	66	66	Delivered as agreed
14	London		72	Commuted sum	Commuted sum paid
15	Yorkshire & Humberside	21	68	14	No data
16	Yorkshire & Humberside	15	600	88	Under construction
17	Yorkshire & Humberside	7	30	2	No data
18	South West	29	14	4	Delivered as agreed
19	South West	19	149	29	Delivered as agreed
20	South West	25	24	6	Delivered as agreed
21	South East	20	50	10	Delivered as agreed
22	South East	26	38	10	Delivered as agreed
23	South East	26	81	21	Delivered as agreed
24	South East	0	39	0	No data
25	North West	17	30	5	No data
26	North West	14	21	3	No data
27	North West	11	81	9	Delivered as agreed
28	South East	16	86	14	No data
29	South East	27	33	9	Delivered as agreed
30	South West	8	5,500	450	Under construction
31	South West	20	100	20	Delivered as agreed
32	West Midlands	10	280	28	Delivered as agreed
33	West Midlands	25	383	96	Delivered as agreed
34	West Midlands	15	100	15 (restricted floorspace)	No data
35	West Midlands	22	46	10	No data
36	East	17	134	23	Under construction
37	East	28	53	15	No data

Delivering affordable housing through Section 106 ————————

Site number	Region	% affordable	Total number of units	Number of affordable units	Affordable housing element of S106
38	East	38	13	5	No data
39	South West	21	61	13	Under construction
40	East		157	Commuted sum	Deed of variation changed affordable on-site to commuted sum
41	London	22	534	116	Change to S106
42	London	25	385	96	Change to S106
43	South East	28	348	96	Delivered as agreed
44	East	11	300	33	Change to tenure without deed of variation
45	East	14	79	11	Delivered as agreed

Appendix 2: The case studies

Introduction

This appendix describes six case studies in detail, focusing on the delivery of the affordable housing element of the S106 agreement. Six case studies were selected to provide a wide range of examples of different S106 developments, in terms of locations, sizes, densities and levels of success in delivering affordable housing. These were: a 157-flat development in the East of England (case 1); a large regeneration scheme in London (case 2); a 534-unit development in London (case 3); a 385-unit development in London (case 4); a 5,500-unit development in the South West (case 5); and a 348-unit development in the South East (case 6). Although, in all the cases, the S106 agreements were honoured by the developers, in a number of them the S106 agreements were renegotiated as circumstances changed. Each case represents a distinct example of the ways in which S106 agreements are affected by changing circumstances within developments.

Case 1 represents a mid-sized development on a brownfield site in a large town. There had been a number of changes throughout the life of the development process. Case study 2 focused on an extremely large and complicated development, but the affordable element was delivered as intended and this provides an example of a well-structured S106.

A former hospital site in London (534 dwellings) was the focus for the development reviewed in case 3 and another former hospital site, also in London (385 dwellings), was the focus for case 4. These two large regeneration sites in London represent examples of the complexities of large sites when they are phased and when subsequently the developer seeks to renegotiate and replan, even when this is done in good faith.

Case 5 was selected because this is a large greenfield development on the edge of a large town. This development is part of the area allocated in the local plan (1999) as a development area. From an affordable housing perspective it can be argued that this development represents a missed opportunity.

Case 6 was a predominantly rural development at a former barracks in the South East. This development has gone ahead as originally planned and is now almost complete, being phased over six periods between 1996 and 2006. It has been used as an 'exemplar' case by those involved and has been on the finalist list for the Deputy Prime Minister's Sustainable Community Awards.

Case study 1

This is an example of a change in the detail of the S106 agreement in which the original requirement of 30 per cent affordable housing to be provided on site was altered to a commuted sum. It also illustrates some of the complexities involved in relation to other planning gain, most of which was also replaced by commuted sums.

The site was originally allocated in the local plan (1996) as a special policy zone for mixed-use development. It is a brownfield site, housing a former warehouse and shops. The whole site abuts the railway line apart from the front, which is on a main road. The original planning application (1999) was for a redevelopment to provide private housing (100 flats – 13 one-bedroom, 79 two-bedroom, eight three-bedroom and including 14 live/work units), affordable housing (33 one-bedroom flats), student housing (300 rooms with two warden flats), fire station, restaurant, health and fitness suite, conference room, community room, commercial/retail space (1,166 square metres – three units) and associated underground car parking, cycle parking, amenity areas, pedestrian and cycle access, servicing and landscaping. This application was approved provided that the affordable units were increased to 40. This was achieved by a proposed conversion of some of the live/work units.

An early variation was made for converting two of the one-bed units into a single three-bed unit, bringing the total of two-bed units to nine.

After detailed consultations, the fire service decided not to relocate to the site. This meant that the fire service provision was changed to a commuted sum of £120,000. The section of the site set aside for the fire station (which is not adjacent to the railway line but is on a main road) was then removed from the application and a separate application made for this now separate site. This was agreed and the commuted sum was paid in 2001.

Further negotiations took place on the development before work started. Other commuted sums were paid for landscaping costs and road costs.

The development of the student housing complex went ahead on the south-east section of the site as set out in the original planning consent. The live/work units were not delivered as originally envisaged. The ground floors of these units were converted to self-contained retail units and the upper floors were converted to separate flats – so, though they remained mixed use, the two uses were separated.

Then, in 2002, there was a deed of variation of schedule 4 of the S106 agreement, which had required the submission and approval of a housing scheme that identified not less than 30 per cent of residential units (excluding the student housing) as affordable housing. The planning committee approved (by four votes to three) the applicant's request that a commuted sum payment be made in place of the on-site provision of affordable housing of £1,765,920. The reason given for this request for a variation was that the service charges attached to the affordable units would be too high. The developer had been in contact with a housing association who agreed that the units were not suitable as affordable housing because of the service charge element.

In the final development, which has now started and some units are complete, there is no restaurant, no fire station, no affordable housing and no community facilities. The developer made an additional commuted sum payment in lieu of the community facilities in 2001, at the same time as the commuted sum paid for the lack of a fire station. Some leisure facilities have been included in the development, but these are for the use of residents only.

The planning department describes the commuted payment for the affordable housing as an 'anomaly'. This situation will not be allowed to arise again and it is felt that the developer has 'got off lightly' in this case. Although the exact location of the affordable elements of the scheme were never formally agreed, it was anticipated by the planners that they would be of similar specification to the market units and would be integrated fully into the scheme. But the leisure facilities were private, not open to the public, but paid for by residents. This made the service charges too high and this is thought to be a major reason for the removal of the affordable housing element. The commuted sum was agreed at 2002 prices but was index-linked, so had increased slightly by the time it was paid. No Social Housing Grant was available for this site. A representative from the local authority noted that it was rare for outline planning permissions not to be taken forward by developers. Where there were differences between permissions granted and development completed, this was because of time lags inherent in the development process.

Case study 2

Outline permission for this development was granted to the developers in 1998 for a mixed-use development. The commercial element of the development incorporates a hotel, gym, retail premises, restaurants and bars, offices, medical facilities and a railway station to provide the transport links. The S106 was signed in May 2000 and included a comprehensive package of affordable housing, transport links and improvements, highways works, education and community contributions and open-space provision.

The development was arranged in three phases. Phase 1 is now complete with 1,065 residential units developed, 515 of which are affordable (although affordable by 2000 definitions). Planning obligations within the S106 relate to each development phase. This brief case study deals with phase 1 of the development and the delivery of affordable housing within that phase.

Full planning permission was granted for phase 1 in 2002. It was made up of an amalgamation of previous detailed approvals, but was subject to the same section 106 agreement as the original outline planning permission. The Mayor of London considered the application on 27 September 2001 and, on 24 January 2002, he allowed the borough council to determine the application following its indication that it was minded to approve planning permission. Blocks C and H of the development were included within the application for 1,065 residential units; 8,032 square metres of B1 floorspace; 6,625 square metres of floorspace for retail, financial and professional services and food and drink; 2,198 square metres of floorspace for non-residential institutions, a 175-bedroom hotel; 3,248 square metres of floorspace for a health and fitness club, a park and riverside walk.

The Mayor wrote to the borough council stating that he supported these proposals subject to securing, through legal agreement, the provision of 505 affordable residential units, the provision of a riverside walk and public park, and securing public transport improvements, namely a contribution towards the proposed railway station, improvements for existing bus services, bus priority and traffic calming measures, and a car parking strategy.

The applicant revised the scheme and on 9 January 2002 the council referred the scheme back to the Mayor for his determination. The council had secured 515 affordable housing units, the provision of the park and a riverside walk. In addition, a package of transport measures had been secured, including increasing the frequency of two bus routes and the extension of a third to the site, a northbound bus lane from the site, and a contribution of £1.75 million towards the provision of a new railway station (a precondition for phase 2 of the outline consent).

In 2002, a further full application, which increased the number of residential units from the original permission was made but was refused by the borough council because of the impact of traffic generation on the highway network; failure to provide the maximum reasonable amount of affordable housing; massing, design and relationship to existing development and proposed park. A modified version of the application was dismissed on appeal in 2003. The maximum reasonable amount of affordable housing would have been defined within the S106 agreement so was required in any subsequent detailed permission.

For phase 1 the original early 2002 permissions were implemented. The 515 affordable units consisted of:

- 275 housing association units for rent

- 75 shared ownership units

- 40 student accommodation units

- 50 key worker units for rent

- 25 key worker units for sale

- 50 frail older people's units for rent.

Phase 1 involved two housing associations. One of them, although not involved in the S106 negotiations, was approached by the local authority in 1999. According to this association, the proportions and size and type of affordable housing have not been altered since the original S106 agreement. There was some SHG used for the rent units on site but no further details were available.

The affordable housing element of the S106 was considered very important during the S106 negotiations. There were certain clauses within the S106 designed to ensure that the originally agreed affordable housing contribution remained intact. These clauses not only provided some certainty for the developer but also ensured that the affordable units were complete in phase 1 before phase 2 could begin.

The affordable housing element of the S106 is extremely detailed. It sets out the process for delivering each of the different affordable tenures and stretches to almost 50 pages. To ensure the completion of the requisite number of affordable units as defined in the S106 agreement, the following clauses were included:

> XXX [developer] shall not permit nor enable any of the private residential units within Development Stage Two to be In Occupation until XXX has received from the Council a written certification stating that at the time of Commencement Stage Two XXX has complied with its obligations under Schedule H Part I [Phase 1 Affordable Housing Obligation] as far as such obligations have arisen having regard to the progress of Development Stage One PROVIDED THAT:-

      1.1.1   The Council shall upon the receipt of a request for such certificate from XXX received at any time after Commencement Stage Two issue such certificate within seven days provided that XXX has substantially complied with its obligations (in so far as such obligations shall have arisen prior to that date) under Schedule H Part I.

Therefore no development may be occupied in phase 2 until the completion of the affordable housing obligation under phase 1. This example shows that, despite a very complex site, permission history and S106 agreement, it is possible for such an agreement to deliver the intended number and tenure of affordable units.

There was a recent appeal over the refusal of the borough council to extend the duration of the outline planning permission. The council claimed that the S106 attached to the outline permissions was outdated and would not supply the type of affordable housing required in the current market, as the negotiations were concluded in 2000. For example, there is the provision for discounted market rental and sale units. The inspectorate granted an extension to the outline permission and determined that the S106 was appropriate and had already successfully delivered affordable housing in phase 1. The deadline for submission of reserved matters applications has been extended to 12 May 2008.

The decision to uphold the contents of the original S106 in this case means that affordable housing negotiated in one particular market cannot be renegotiated by the local authority because of changing market circumstances and a desire that the affordable contribution should reflect the changes in housing need. The borough council was unable to change the agreement for discounted market rent and sale units, which may have been affordable in the 2000 housing market but are not affordable in the current market.

Case study 3

This large regeneration site in London is an example of the complexities of large sites when they are phased and when subsequently the developer seeks to renegotiate and replan the scheme. However, while the local authority took a clear stance on what it wanted out of the S106 agreement, it was prepared to renegotiate providing this involved an increase in the affordable housing contribution. This was largely because the proportion of affordable housing was raised to 35 per cent in the new unitary development plan (UDP), which was changing over the life of the site.

This site is on its third replan, each with a deed of variation. It was allocated in the UDP but it has a long history. The original outline planning permission (granted in 1996 for the whole site) dates back to a previous plan policy where the affordable housing contribution was a lower percentage of the total. It is a large brownfield site (a hospital redevelopment) and construction was always going to be phased. It is located in one of the cheaper parts of London and, as the developer has been building and selling, evidence has shown that there is a strong and continuing demand for smaller properties, which come onto the market at relatively affordable prices in the London context. So each replan reflects this, as the developer responds to the demand by increasing the numbers of smaller units in the scheme. This implies an adjustment in the S106 agreement.

The total number of units on the current phase of the site is 534, of which considerably less than the current UDP target of 35 per cent are affordable, because the original planning consent was for only 20 per cent affordable (agreed under a former UDP). However, there is 35 per cent on the 'uplift' (the additional units resulting from building at a higher density than originally planned). The total affordable units for the development are 116 (21.7 per cent): 51 are one-bed flats; 40 are two-bed; four are three-bed; and 21 are houses.

This site is thus an example of changing the S106 agreement by degrees. There have been two applications from the developer to change the mix and type of units, which would have triggered a greater number of affordable units, although the percentage would have been the same as in the original agreement. However, because the percentage target in the UDP had changed, the local authority also wished to renegotiate, in order to achieve 35 per cent affordable housing. The original planning permission started off with 442 dwellings, the second application increased this to 493 and the current agreement is 534. Each time the increase was achieved by building more one-bed units and fewer two- and three-bed units.

The main factors taken into account on these two reapplications were issues of design and the effect that the increase in density has on the local authority's design principles. Other aspects that were considered were the impact on neighbouring properties, the impact on car parking, changing residential mix and air quality (linked to the potential increases in traffic). It is a design-led scheme. There were no issues linked to higher costs on a brownfield site, as it was low-cost reclamation.

In terms of the integration of the affordable housing on the site, all the houses on the site (as opposed to the flats) are affordable and part of an existing residential street. There is a block of flats where there is a mix of affordable and market, but different service arrangements. Other blocks are not integrated in this way. The affordable housing tends to be concentrated in one side of the site, but there is no easily distinguishable difference in quality, materials or design between the market and the affordable units. There are two housing associations involved on the site.

The local authority also looked at the rail and bus links around the site, which is within easy walking distance of the main railway station. The S106 agreement included sums for environmental improvements and the council is looking at development opportunities in that area, as 'there may be £20,000 left over for environmental improvements.' Other planning gain included the restoration of a Victorian water tower on the site and the retention of the nicer hospital buildings, which were refurbished for community uses, including a doctor's surgery and a day nursery. All this was funded through the S106.

This local authority takes a 'hard' negotiating stance and has the full support of council members. The planners feel the main thing about any development is that the authority is clear about what contributions are required. They expect the landowner (in this case the health authority) to 'take a hit' when negotiating with the developer, otherwise the developer has to take a hit on their profit margins. Where sites have unusually high costs the authority has to set a balance, taking all competing claims on planning gain into account. The developers do protest against the affordable housing contribution and their view is that the social housing is not being maintained as well as the market housing so it looks untidy and there is litter around. But, when they were negotiating the increase in density and total numbers, they accepted that they would not get permission for the increase without meeting the 35 per cent requirements in the UDP.

This site is being monitored by regular site visits by the planning department to check on completions and handover to the housing association. It is a continuing site with further phases to be completed. The planners have been told by the housing department that Social Housing Grant cannot be used on S106 sites, as this is local policy. So all the affordable housing is funded by the developer contribution plus private finance (loans) on the part of the housing association.

Case study 4

This is similar to case study 3 as it too involves a hospital redevelopment. It is thus a large site, subject to phasing, and the developer wished to renegotiate in order to increase the number of units in total. They were happy to provide the 25 per cent affordable housing UDP target, which then resulted in additional affordable units.

However, the Greater London Council tried to impose 50 or 35 per cent on the additional units (the original permission was for 341, which then became 385) but they are all 25 per cent of the total (as in the local plan).

This development is now almost complete. It comprises two elements – the main hospital site and the west wing (maternity hospital) site. The main site has been completed and the new road is just being completed now. On the west wing site all the houses and flats have been built and only a hotel remains to be completed. It is a mixed-use development, with the provision of commercial units and the hotel, which is seen as an employment site. The affordable housing is 'pepper potted' throughout the housing elements of the development.

Social Housing Grant was made available for the development and all of the affordable housing was built to the standards set out by the Housing Corporation, both in terms of density and quality. The developer noted that these standards can often be in excess of what a developer would normally provide for market housing and/or result in differences to the units. The developer did note, however, that the affordable housing was ostensibly the same as the market housing provided in this instance.

S106 agreements are now a major cost factor in developments for the developer of this scheme, with the developer spending £1m a month on the delivery of S106 commitments. On this site and others the developer is clear (as are other large developers interviewed) that S106 agreements are quite easily enforceable through the courts. The interviewee had never heard of a case where a developer failed to deliver what was on an S106 agreement. Even renegotiations were difficult and there had to be a good reason for changes to S106 agreements. It would be irresponsible of a developer, from a business perspective, to fail to deliver what was set out on an S106 – primarily because the developer would then be leaving themselves open to future problems and inherent bad publicity.

The site was allocated as a redevelopment site in the UDP as part of a growth point but was not specifically identified for housing. There were three parties to the S106 negotiations – the landowner (Department of Health), the developer and the council. The price paid for the land will have taken account of the planning gain including the affordable housing, implying that the landowner bore much of the burden of S106 agreements in this case.

Other S106 commitments made by the developer consisted of a community building, a contribution towards a cycle way to the north of the site, a contribution to education and contributions to enhance the memorial gardens, highway works and a play area.

Case study 5

This development is part of the area allocated in the local plan as a development area. In the revised deposit draft plan (October 2003) this is described as a 261-hectare greenfield location on the northern edge of the town. The development is not yet completed, but the Section 106 agreement is being delivered as agreed, with the development consortium in the process of building all the housing, prior to the transfer of some of it to the relevant housing associations. At the end of 2005 the total number of occupations was 1,802, but the local authority had given approval for 3,333 occupations, out of a total of 5,500 – implying that the development was nearing completion.

This represents a major new greenfield development for the town. Four-hundred-and-fifty of the units are to be affordable, with 45 for low-cost home ownership (shared ownership) and 405 for rent. Affordable housing thus represents 8 per cent of the total housing on this development and provides a poor comparison with other percentages negotiated elsewhere. The development is also split between a number of different developers, which are part of an overall consortium. Each developer is responsible for a separate part of the development, although it is clear that the developers negotiated with the local authority via the consortium. This has meant that individual developers have dealt with individual housing associations, to deliver affordable housing – confusing the overall situation. Six different housing associations are involved.

The district council's revised deposit draft plan 2003 (RDDP) shies away from a 30 per cent affordable housing target on sites of 0.5 hectares or more, or on sites of 15 units or more (as set out in an earlier draft plan). Instead the RDDP (2003, p. 127, 5.5.13) states:

> ... there are concerns amongst both developers and the [consortium] that regenerative efforts may be constrained if the current 30 per cent target for affordable housing is rigidly insisted upon.

Despite this, the local authority does have an affordable housing officer and it has been noted that affordable strategies and S106 agreements have improved dramatically since the scheme was agreed.

None of the affordable housing on the site will be for 100 per cent sub-market sale. Some Social Housing Grant is being used to fund the development of the affordable housing and the affordable housing is being totally integrated within the overall development. The affordable housing is also considerably varied, with a number of semi-detached houses, detached houses, terraces and flats – of different sizes. Of the 53 units to be managed by one housing association (for example), it was noted that four will be for key worker shared ownership (with a 50/50 rent/purchase split on each). The rest of the housing will be for rent. The affordable housing is to be totally integrated within the overall development. The affordable housing is built to the quality and density standards set out by the Housing Corporation and is designed to be externally indistinguishable from the market housing on the site.

The local authority has nomination rights for the affordable housing on the site, but the quality of all of the new housing developments around the town has been called into question. In a BBC report (5 January 2006) it was noted that the town's new developments had been compared to prisons.

Case study 6

The main interview for this study was with the housing association. The site has been used as an 'exemplar' case by those involved and has been on the finalist list for the Deputy Prime Minister's Sustainable Community Awards. This development is now almost complete, although some final work is currently being undertaken.

The 57-acre site was earmarked for development in the district council's 2001 local plan, although permission had already been given for the development of the site in 1999, when it was released by the Ministry of Defence. The total of 348 dwellings was to represent a major housing development for the district and was seen as fulfilling a large element of its new-build housing target (set out in the county structure plan). The development of the site was phased over six periods between 1999 and 2006.

The scheme was designed by a community planning architect on 'urban village' principles, with a 'pepper-potted' mix of tenures and a mixture of uses – and with the involvement of the local community from the initial planning stage. It is a redevelopment of a 57-acre, former Ministry of Defence barracks. Previously home to Guards Regiments, who vacated the site in 1995, the barracks have been transformed into a new community called 'The Village'. Social Housing Grant was made available for all 96 affordable housing units (27.5 per cent of the total development) at 100 per cent TCI net of on-costs. The S106 agreement ensured that the TCI levels used were those relating to the year in which the development was to commence.

The total value of the project exceeds £60 million and includes business accommodation, a business enterprise centre, retail and commercial space, 12 live and work units, health and leisure facilities, day nursery and childcare, 348 housing units, a community farm, bus service and a nursing home. An S106 agreement was signed for the development, whereby the developer agreed that 96 units would be affordable. All have been delivered. Seventy-eight are for rent, nine are for shared ownership and the remainder were sub-market sale. Tenants are nominated by the local authority area in which the site is based. The affordable properties are managed by a single housing association. Note that affordable housing is pepper potted, but that this has been arranged to avoid high service costs.

Some of the affordable housing is flats. A typical one-bedroom flat would have a monthly rent of £274.34, plus mortgage repayments on £78,500 (equating to a 50/50 split). This would result in a monthly cost of around £700 per month. A typical two-bedroom flat would have a monthly rent of £320.75, plus mortgage repayments on £94,000 (representing a purchase of a 50 per cent share). This would result in a monthly cost of around £900 per month.

Many of the community facilities in the village are conversions of former barracks facilities. These include a restored cricket ground; the chapel and gymnasium are being converted to community uses – private health and fitness club, restaurant/cafe bar. The sergeants' mess has already been converted to a veterinary surgery and other community facilities planned include a community farm and nature reserve, children's play area and skateboard/rollerblading park.

The developer's contributions (via payment and in kind) include:

- £30,000 for the restoration of the cricket square

- £500,000 for the bus service

- £200 bus vouchers for each household

- £50,000 for off-site transport improvements

- £250,000 for the community trust

- £100,000 to the local education authority

- £950,000 for the retention and refurbishment of period buildings, intended for community use.

Summary

The six case study developments provide an overview of the possibilities when S106 agreements are used to deliver affordable housing. Density and quality tend to reflect the density and quality of the overall developments and there is little evidence of high levels of segregation between market and affordable units in the cases examined here. Failure is typified in cases 1 and 5. In the former, this failure was linked to poor planning and negotiation at the early stages of the development process, although the quality of the overall development is considered high. In case 5, the failure was linked to the relatively poor quality of the overall development, set in a background environment of an inadequate and badly supported local plan (a commitment to 30 per cent affordable housing has even been removed from the latest draft of the local plan), a strong developer position (a consortium of developers negotiated) and generally low expectations (the Mayor's comments being one example of this). Cases 3 and 4 illustrate strong local planning strategies on affordable housing, coupled with an overall push on this issue by the Greater London Authority (GLA). Case 6 represents one of the more successful examples of the judicious use of S106 agreements to deliver affordable housing targets, although the site and general conditions clearly made this more practicable than in many of the other cases examined. For case 2, the S106 delivered affordable housing as intended but is now considered not to reflect current housing need. The local authority wants to renegotiate but the original agreements were reinforced at appeal. Interviewees from planning departments noted that it was rare for outline planning permissions not to be taken forward by developers. Where there were differences between permissions granted and development completions, this was because of time lags inherent in the development process.